The Ultimate Guide to Planning an Outdoor Wedding

SÁMI
TIPI

Stunning Tipis, Unforgettable Events

Craig Bidder & Jodie Bidder

About the Authors

Craig and Jodie Bidder are the owners of the award winning Sami Tipi providing stunning tipi hire for all kinds of inspired events.

"Our love of tipis and the beginning of our outdoor wedding experience started in 2012 and we have been on an amazing journey since, helping wonderful couples celebrate the outdoor wedding of their dreams.

In this book we want to share our knowledge and experience and hope that you can use it as your planning bible to help you along the way to your amazing day".

Craig & Jodie

Dedication

We are extremely grateful to those who have been a part of
our amazing journey...

Our parents and close friends who have supported
us every step of the way.

All of those talented industry friends who have contributed
to our lives, and this book.

And to our amazing kids Harry and Poppy who have had to
put up with a bonkers mum and dad along the way.

Thank you all

CONTENTS

Pop in a gorgeous selfie of the two of you here

The Most AMAZING Decision You Will Make

1. Introduction

The most amazing decision you will make

Having an outdoor wedding is a spectacular way to celebrate your marriage. A magical day, uniquely created by you in a breathtaking setting that simply cannot be re-created indoors.

An outdoor wedding allows you the flexibility to have the day you want and not the traditional conveyor belt wedding. How the day will look and feel are your choices and not dictated by anyone else.

An outdoor wedding, really...?

You may get a lot of family or friends that just do not understand the awesome decision you have taken to make your day uniquely yours by having an outdoor wedding. Accept now that people will think that you are bonkers, we promise you that by the end of your big day everyone will understand why you did and will be talking about it for years to come.

"Some people think that having an outdoor wedding is a cheaper option. That isn't necessarily the case, but what you can get is a more unique wedding rather than a package, generic wedding where another couple the week before have had the exact same day in a different colour. Outdoor weddings give you the flexibility to have the day how you want it".

Not a budget option

Most people have the pre-conceived idea that having an outdoor wedding is an easier, lower budget option. Not wanting to burst your bubble this early on but this is usually not the case, however the time and money spent leading up to your big day will pay you back with the most amazing memories, not only for you but your guests alike and you will not regret that decision!

Just because an outdoor wedding isn't a budget option, doesn't mean that you can't work to a budget, you will just need to be realistic with the time and costs involved. From the very beginning work out how much you can afford or at least how much you want to spend, find out whether family are going to help out financially but beware of the 'strings attached' to this, such as a requirement to invite all of your long lost relatives.

Consider how much you can save between now and the wedding day. To help plan for this we have included a budget planner on page 136.

A handy guide

This book has been designed to be a handy guide to help you through the process of planning your outdoor wedding and keeping all of your ideas together as a working file.

It includes useful tips, quotes and knowledge from wedding industry experts involved in outdoor weddings and actual couples (ones who have!) who have already created their own outdoor wedding memories.

Of course you are welcome to read all of this book now from cover to cover, but use it as a workbook, read the sections and tips again when you reach that point in your planning process.

In this book we give you an understanding of the details involved in planning your outdoor wedding. This may seem daunting at first but our advice is to embrace the process and make sure you enjoy every part of it. These are happy times so allow yourself to dream big, be creative, go on YOUR OWN journey and most of all, have FUN!

15

A place to dream about your day

Your
DATE

2. Your Date

So you have decided to have an outdoor wedding, the first thing to consider is your date. Once you have a date in mind, ask yourself how important is your date to you? Well of course it is going to be important as it is your wedding day, but is there any significance to the date you have chosen?

What we actually mean by this is are you getting married on a special date such as an anniversary or birthday? Limiting your date to one possibility can be restrictive especially if you are planning last minute.

For those of you that are super organised and are planning your wedding well in advance you shouldn't have a problem securing your ideal date, however if not, being open minded can help with securing your first choice suppliers.

The key components

For any outdoor wedding there are three key components that need to come together in the first instance:

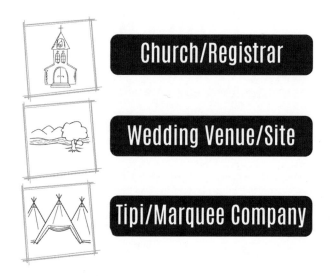

What is your number one priority?

In an ideal world you would be able to secure all three of the key components on the date you have chosen but if not you may need to prioritise which one means the most to you and compromise on the others, this is where the date flexibility really helps. Churches generally hold only one wedding per day so if this is important to you and have your heart set on a specific one, this should be your first enquiry.

Chicken or the egg...

Which do you book first, the venue or your tipi/marquee company?

You may be lucky enough to have a few acres tucked away behind your family home or be best friends with a local farmer. If however you are looking at popular wedding venues, these can be booked up to a year or more in advance.

Most established tipi/marquee companies can cater for more than one wedding per week but the good ones can also get booked up early.

You will have to make a choice about which is more important to you, the venue or a particular tipi/marquee company. This will identify which one needs booking first. Again this is where your date flexibility comes in as this could be the difference between securing all of your first choice suppliers (church, venue, tipi/marquee company) or having to make a compromise. Peak dates for weddings are always Spring Bank Holiday in May and the summer school holidays so if your date falls within these times, get in early.

Scribble Space

Seasonal considerations

The season that you choose to hold your outdoor wedding will have a significant effect on the feel of your day. An outdoor wedding can be magical at any time of the year and each season brings its own set of challenges. With a spring or autumn wedding, heating should be a consideration as whilst temperatures may be great in the day, they will drop off in the evening. (see chapter 5, The Boring Bits, for more details). This could also have an effect on how your tipi/marquee are set up as you may wish to close them up more to help keep in the heat.

Extending your day

The bonus of having this style of wedding is that you are in control of the length of your celebration. Gone are the days of a standard ceremony followed by a traditional wedding breakfast, a few moves on the dance floor then home by midnight (although this is still perfectly fine). Instead you have the opportunity to extend the wedding to a weekend celebration.

TOP TIP

Camping provides cost effective accommodation for your guests, no taxis required and you get to enjoy breakfast the following morning.

Your tipi/marquee and land hire may last for a period of around 3-4 days giving you the chance to implement your unique styling ideas before the wedding day and then continue the partying through the night with guests stopping over and then enjoying breakfast or a bbq lunch together the next day. Some of your guests may have travelled a long way to help celebrate your special day. Extending your wedding will give you extra time to spend with these family and friends.

Another bonus of having your guests with you the following day is that you will have more hands available to help with any clearing away!

Your Guest Numbers

You may ask why we would mention this so early on in the process. Well by having a rough idea on your numbers, this will help you to plan the space you need for your tipi/marquee structure and will allow you to get an accurate quotation based on your actual requirements. You can always refine the numbers later on but this magic number will ultimately define the cost of your event.

TOP TIP
Would you buy them dinner tomorrow? Have you had dinner with them in the last year? If yes then they are in!

Your 'furry' best friend

One of the benefits of having an outdoor wedding is that you can extend your guest list to these other important family members 'the furry variety'.

Your outdoor space gives them freedom to run around and be a part of your day too.

Make arrangements with a local pet stay or dog walker company to collect them after your ceremony and photos as just like small children, they may become overwhelmed. Dont forget to take a bowl, water and lead for them.

Photo credit: Yvonne Lishman Photography

26

Photo credit: Matt Brown Photography

Guest List Selector

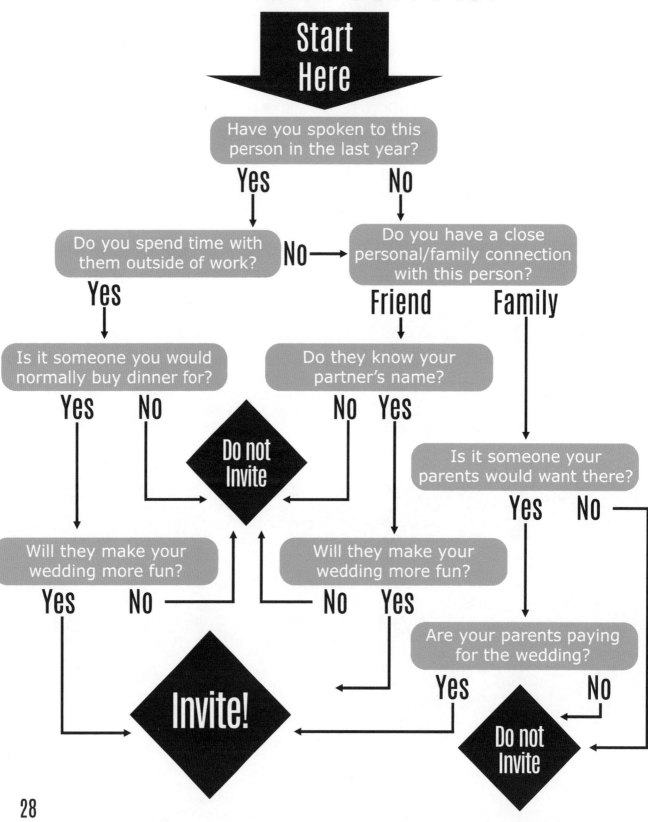

Top Tips to conquer your Seating Plan

This can be one of the toughest parts of wedding planning but the tips below will help to make it a little less painful.

• DO start early. It will take more time than you think to get right. If you are having a printed version on display try not to send it to print until as late as possible, as there will always be last minute changes.

• DON'T feel that you have to stick to traditional round tables of 8 or 10. Having long rectangular tables can help everyone to feel important. These work perfectly in a tipi. Consider what works best with your space and style.

• DO consider table names. Numbers make people think there is an order of importance so naming tables after important places or events can work much better.

• DO invest in Post-It notes. Write all guests names on a Post-It and move them around a drawing of your seating plan, this is so much quicker and less scribbling out than if you write them on directly. Alternatively download software such as Tablerrr or Top Table Planner to keep it all online, in one place.

- DON'T struggle to keep all friendship groups together, it might get a bit cliquey and harder to split equally over tables so mixing it up can be lots of fun. Try to put a couple of people who know each other on the same table just to help get conversation going.

- DO sit young children with their parents. If you have a lot of older children they might like to sit together on a children's table. Consider the location of small children and babies – a table that is near to the door is easier for parents to take any mischief makers outside, especially during the speeches.

- DO make it clear to your caterer where guests with special diets are seated. Colour coding their copy of the seating plan and even putting a coloured dot on place cards to highlight any different meals will help the waiting staff immensely.

- DON'T feel that you have to stick to tradition for your top table. Especially if you have step-parents, multiple bridesmaids or important family members who you would love to sit on the top table.

Supplied by Thomas the Caterer

Seating Plan

Mr & Mrs ...

Table One
Charlotte Smith
Layla Smith
Erin Smith
Bernard Downing
Emily Allsopp
Lucy Sticks
Karl Sticks

Table Two
Adam Wright
Rebecca Wright
Jules King
Kitty King
Keelin Barker
Kris Barker
Darran Downie
John Headley

Table Three
Marie Barker
Paul Barker
Amy Totem
Orlee Totem
Laura Totem
Greg Totem
Pete Campbell
Chris Campbell

Table Four
Anja Hilderbrant
Steve Ellis
Sally Ellis
Jade Kyle
Vicky Longton
Rachel Williams
Jenny Ryan
Jenny Ryan

Table Five
Amy Keegan
Tom Wattemore
Carl Allen
Rhys Allen
Shaun Allen
Sarah Stevens
Ross Sticks
Leanne Wright

Table Six
Abby Beevers
Sharon Totem
Stephen Totem
Joy Totem
Jeff Totem
Tina Totem
Hilary Campbell
Jenson Campbell

Table Seven
Gary Sticks
Lynne Sticks
Brian Allsopp
Judy Allsopp
Jack Allsopp
Sam Allsopp
Colette Sticks

Table Eight
Jim Clare
Ernie Brown
Julie Brown
John Sticks
Liam Sticks
James Sticks
Kath Sticks

Finding the LAND

3. Finding the Land

Finding the perfect site can seem like a challenge in itself. When deciding on your location or site, consider how do you want your day to look and feel? This could help in deciding on the type of site you choose to host your outdoor wedding celebration.

First and foremost consider what kind of site you would like, what is important to you?

Would you prefer a farmer's field, a woodland setting, a site close to water or something in the grounds of a stately home?

Sometimes the decision is led by budget as ground hire can range from £100's upwards into the £1000's, so have yourself a budget allocation for this purpose.

TOP TIP

Don't be put off by a higher venue price as the added value might be worth its weight in gold.

Often farmers are looking to diversify and will happily hire out a field, and there really can be some gems out there. The tipi/marquee companies that you are considering may have a venue page on their website or have sites they have worked with previously that can be recommended to you.

But how do you find these sites?

Our advice would be to put the word out to family and friends. Facebook is often a good starting point for this, asking people if they know of anywhere.

Google maps provides a very clever mapping service too. If you know roughly the region you are looking to locate a suitable site in, search for maps.google.co.uk

On the mapping screen there is an option to "search" where you can enter what you would like to locate, i.e. farm, holiday lodge etc. Google will then pin the results for you and if there is a website or contact details available these will also be listed making it easy to contact the owner.

TOP TIP

A top tip is to look at potential sites at the time of year you are going to get married. Trees, grass, plants and flowers will look very different throughout the year and may dramatically change the feeling of your wedding day.

Photo credit: Yvonne Lishman Photography

35

This tool is perfect for searching many different styles of sites. Bed and breakfasts and holiday lodges can make for a perfect setting, providing guests that are travelling a place to stay as well as offering you the perfect wedding venue.

The possibilities are endless, it just needs a little time and research. Other examples may be boating lakes, cafes, zoos, schools, forestry parks, sporting clubs, old train stations, campsites, caravan parks. What we are trying to say is it is always important to keep open minded and think outside of the box.

How do you know if a site is suitable?

From a logistical point of view, your site will need to be accessible for large vehicles for the event setup. There needs to be enough flat ground for the tipi/marquee structure plus any room you need outside of this space.

Also look out for overhead cables and underground services, which the land owner should be able to advise on.

Site Essentials
- Flat area for tipis/marquee ✓
- Good vehicle access ✓
- Privacy ✓
- Power connection (nice to have) ✓
- Water connection (nice to have) ✓
- On site toilets (nice to have) ✓
- Plenty of parking ✓

Comparing Different Sites
- Is event management offered?
- Are they there on the day?
- How often can you visit the site before hand?
- As a venue, do they offer planning meetings?
- How long is the hire period?
- Do they have their own ceremony room?
- Do they work with preferred suppliers or are you free to use who you wish?
- Do they provide a bar/or catering?
- Is camping allowed?
- What is the cut off time for music?
- Are fireworks allowed?
- What is and isn't included in the price?

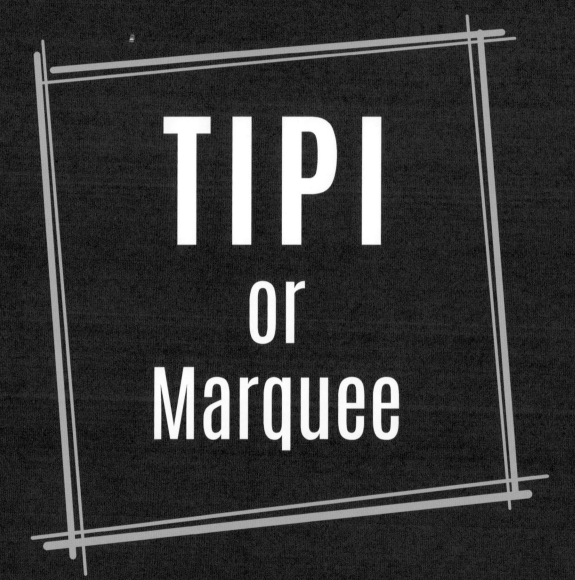

TIPI
or
Marquee

4. Tipi or Marquee

Armed with your guest numbers, an idea of geographical location and preferred season/month, you can now start to think about the type of structure you would like to celebrate in.

Choosing the right structure

If you have already fallen in love with a certain site or piece of land then your choice of structure will be influenced by this. It may be that your venue has its own tipi or marquee in which case the decision will be made for you. If you are choosing your own structure you need to consider the space that your venue has to accommodate this.

TOP TIP

Finding a good quality tipi/marquee supplier will make planning your outdoor wedding so much easier.

Photo credit: Richard Murgatroyd Photography

Structure options:

- Tipi
- Stretch tent
- Marquee
  - o Capri
  - o Sperry
  - o Clear span
  - o Inflatable
- Circus tent
- Yurt
- Arabian tent

When choosing your structure you need to consider the following:

What structure best represents your personalities?

What type of structure is more inkeeping with the natural surroundings?

What is going to be more appropriate for the time of year you are getting married?

Once you have narrowed your choices down to a few options, the next question is which one is more inkeeping with your budget? You may not know the answer to this one so the next step is to request quotations from selected suppliers.

Requesting quotations and choosing a supplier

You should now be ready to request quotations for your tent structure. Contact three reputable companies for quotations, ask them about their optional extras, so that when they put a quotation together for you, everything is included. This way you can see the total price and not just a low one that you have to keep adding to. Items such as fairy lights, dance floor, catering annex, table and chair options and even a sparkly disco ball should be itemised on your quotation. You can always remove items before committing to a booking. It can be difficult sometimes to compare your quotes like for like, don't be afraid to ask your more expensive suppliers where their added value is, it may be worth the extra few pounds.

Photo credit: Richard Murgatroyd Photography

Confirm what else is included in your price. Will you receive ongoing support, planning meetings, floor planning discussions etc. This will allow you to make a more informed decision about which company is best suited for you to work with.

There are plenty of photos and videos showcasing tipis and marquees all over the internet but there is no comparison to actually seeing and experiencing them for yourself. If you have never seen a tipi or marquee ask if they have any open events coming up or if they are set up locally for an event so that you can go and see the structure before making a firm decision.

When requesting your quotations from your tipi/marquee suppliers make sure you confirm your hire period.

Photo credit: Richard Murgatroyd Photography

Does this fit with your land hire period or do you need to extend one or the other to allow you to celebrate your event over the whole weekend? There may be additional costs to this so work out exactly how long you need.

Your structure is a big part of your day, you will be working closely with the company that you choose for a considerable amount of time whilst planning your wedding. Make sure you choose a company that you trust and ultimately like and feel comfortable asking lots of questions of. Good relationships are critical when dealing with your big day.

Ask to see testimonials or even speak to past clients and find out if the company are a member of an industry trade association such as MUTA which means that they will follow industry-leading best practice giving you more peace of mind.

Your choice of supplier might also be influenced by their choice of optional extras and special touches. These will help to enhance your big day and make the event space more unique and unforgettable.

> ## TOP TIP - Sizing Up!
> Once you have your structure booked ask for measurements of tables, benches, chairs, poles etc. This will help you to plan and create all of your DIY touches such as bunting, table runners, hanging ribbons on chairs etc

45

Security of your structure

Remember that the tipis/marquee and all of the equipment that are in them are your responsibility once they are handed over to you. Depending on the location of your site it may be worth investing in security for the duration of your hire. Your two options are:

1. Hire in a security company to patrol your site or even just visit hourly throughout the nights before your wedding.

2. You or some of your friends could camp on site for a few days leading up to the day.

It is advisable to take out wedding insurance that also covers the tipis/marquee. Most wedding insurers will inclide this option but you will need to find out from your supplier what value of cover needs to be taken.

Photo credit: Richard Murgatroyd Photography

DANCING SHOES

You bought new shoes to match your dress
And now your feet are quite a mess.
But don't sit down and admit defeat.
Kick off your heels and enjoy this treat!

TOP TIP
Provide flip flops for your guests. They'll love them and it prevents your beautiful dress being stood on by high heels!

The BORING Bits

5. The Boring Bits

The Boring Bits That Make Your Outdoor Wedding Function

Your outdoor venue may have stunning natural beauty, but does it have electricity for your lighting and caterers, toilet facilities for your guests and adequate parking? If it has then this is a bonus and one thing ticked off the list already. However if like most outdoor wedding venues these are not present then do not worry, these are easily sorted with the right knowledge and support.

You've got the power!

In order for your outdoor wedding celebration to happen it is going to need electricity, if there is none on site, you will need to hire a generator.

But what size generator will you need? This largely depends on your caterers, as these will be the ones using the most amount of power. We would always recommend getting a larger kVa than is required as you do not want your party to come to a standstill and the lights go out. As a rule, for an outdoor wedding of up to 120 guests a 40kVa generator should do the job.

The generator will be positioned away from the tipis, but still ensure that it is a super silent one, as they do still generate some noise.

Photo credit: Yvonne Lishman Photography

The cost of your generator has a number of variables, such as delivery charges, fuel consumption on the day and the size of generator you hire.

When planning your "set up timeline" (see page 133) ensure that the generator will be delivered on the same day as your tipi/marquee structure as your tipi/marquee supplier will need to check that their lighting is working correctly and this means they will need to have access to a suitable power supply. This could be a temporary connection taken from a house or garage socket if your generator is not yet available.

In some cases your tipi/marquee supplier may source the generator for you or even have their own.

How to choose a generator

Firstly, list your suppliers and then confirm with them if they actually need power.

Once you have established if they require an electric connection find out what it is they are powering and the output they need.

If your caterer is preparing a three course meal with hot plates and using tea urns the power demand will be

higher and consume a large chunk of your generator's power in contrast to a hog roast or BBQ which require no electrical power at all.

As a rule, most lighting in tipis/marquees will be LED so will require minimal power.

Event generators generally come in sizes 10kVa, 20kVa, 30kVa, 40kVa, 60kVa and upwards. For most weddings the 40kVa would be more than adequate however there is often a very minor price difference between the sizes and so for a small extra cost you could go for the larger event generator and have the peace of mind that everything is more than covered.

Photo credit: Yvonne Lishman Photography

Supplier	Do they need Power?	What are they Powering?	Plug Type	Output
Tipi/Marquee Supplier	✓	Lights, mirror ball	2x 16amp	5kW

Once you have compiled this information you can provide it to your generator company or tipi/marquee company to help them size the generator, and advise on what equipment you need.

| Standard 13amp plug | 16amp plug | 32amp plug (3 pin) | 32amp plug (5 pin) |

Other things to consider when booking the Generator:

You may need to book more equipment than just the generator. Confirm with your tipi/marquee company if they will provide any distribution boxes and plug points within the structure for you and your suppliers to use. If not you will have to request these from you generator company.

As overwhelming as this all may sound, we promise it is not and any good generator company or tipi/marquee company will have years of experience in dealing with this and will guide you through the process.

Another consideration is whether to have call-out cover or a second generator. It is highly unlikely that anything will go wrong with the generator, however it might be cost effective to have a backup one just in case. It is always a good question to ask the generator company costings for both options.

Generators run on red diesel so remember just like a car they can run out of fuel. If the generator is used only on your wedding day there should be no issues at all however if you have it running for 2-3 days before the wedding running chillers etc. get a groomsman to double check the fuel level on the morning

of the wedding and top it up if required. You can ask your generator company to show you how to do this.

Hiring in toilets

When hiring in toilets for your event there are two options available to you, the traditional portaloo or the more favoured luxury toilet block.

TOP TIP
Book a toilet unit that your guests are going to be happy using.

Photo credit: Yvonne Lishman Photography

These can be very stylish inside with many little features like colour changing lights and music. Consider maybe hiring a disabled unit, not necessarily because anyone needs it for this purpose but because it provides you with a larger area to freshen up in and space for a baby changing unit if required. Keep some toiletry items in here to ensure you are as fresh as a daisy throughout the whole day.

Many toilet hire companies can also provide you with shower units, if you are considering extending the celebration and camping over.

Photo credit: Yvonne Lishman Photography

Rubbish and recycling

Depending upon your venue and their stipulations, something else to consider is the removal of rubbish. A simple way of removing rubbish from site is either by contacting the local council and paying for a special collection or hiring in a mini skip, which can always be hidden. If this is not possible it is all hands on deck the following day, roping in your family and friends to help clear away the rubbish and then take it to your local recycling centre.

Lighting the way to the carpark

Your generator company may also hire out lighting towers, which could be used to light up the car parking area. Providing your guests with a safely lit pathway from your event field to the car parking area is a must.

You can mark out a walkway to your car parking area with garden solar lights or by using shepherds hooks and lanterns, or even light the pathway with battery tea lights in jam jars, which is really effective as well as looking fabulous.

Photo credit: Matt Brown

Will your tipis/marquee require heating?

During the summer months you should not require a heater, when the evening temperature dips guests can always warm up by a gorgeous indoor fireplace (only available in tipis). During September through to May, it would be advisable to have heating. Blow heaters require diesel and electricity and will arrive with a full tank of fuel. This would be available to hire from your tipi/marquee company or the generator supplier.

If the temperature is of concern to you, for peace of mind request a quotation for the hire of a heater and add this into you overall budget. The final decision can usually be made on the week of the wedding when you know what the forecast is for your big day.

Photo credit: Matt Brown Photography

Logistics/parking

The importance of parking can sometimes be overlooked and so for a small effort you can avoid cars parking in the wrong field or even driving over your perfectly manicured bowling green garden.

You will need to decide and plan where your wedding guests are going to park their cars. Work on the basis of 2 persons to a car so with 200 guests you may have up to 100 cars.

Clear signage is a must and can be made cheaply and effectively with offcuts of wood painted with chalkboard paint.

You may be lucky enough to have a spare field to park your cars. Just make sure it is well lit and that in the event of wet weather it won't get too boggy, leaving everyone stuck. If you don't have a large field for parking guests, then you could look at local establishments such as pubs or even a village hall and then provide a bus transfer to the wedding. This option for parking can open up a large range of venues that you previously thought were too small.

Don't forget that your 'on the day' wedding suppliers will need to park at the actual wedding venue for some or all of the day. These may include your caterer (who may even have a van or a minibus for staff), bar company, photographer, florist, band etc.

All parking arrangements should be planned and organised well in advance and your guests should be advised as to where to park on their wedding invitations. You could use the services of one or more of your ushers to show guests where to park on the day.

If you have any elderly or disables guests attending your wedding, you should consider giving priority spaces for these.

If your wedding field is remote or not easy to locate why not post a few signs, balloons or even decorated garden spades along the route. Remember a map is great to get guests to the site but these details ensure smooth running on the day. Remember to add this to the list of tasks.

The WEATHER

6. The Weather

We all know the unpredictability of the British summer but don't let this dampen your spirits, as it is completely out of your control. You need to embrace the elements and with a few planning ideas you can sit back, relax and just enjoy whatever is thrown at you.

Photo credit: Yvonne Lishman Photography

Make sure you have a Plan B

Having a Plan B for an outdoor wedding is a must. Think about what impact different kinds of weather might have. You may have the most beautiful sunny day, however having a few back-up plans in place can allow you to relax and enjoy your day knowing every outcome is dealt with.

Keep your timings flexible so that in the event of a sudden downpour just before the ceremony you can delay it until the sun comes back out, alternatively make sure you have enough indoor space so that, at the drop of a hat, you can move the whole ceremony indoors.

Have alternative hard standing parking facilities in case the field you were planning to use becomes waterlogged or muddy.

Consider your guests

Think about the time of year you are planning to hold your wedding and what the weather may be like.

For a summer event you may want to consider having bottles of cold water to hand to keep your guests hydrated. Think about where your ceremony will be held so that the sun is shining on peoples backs not directly into their eyes. You could even hand out pretty paper fans to help guests keep cool and don't forget a bottle of sun tan lotion for those who may have forgotten, the British sun can burn at times!

If there is a possibility of rain it is worth considering supplying a basket full of fancy umbrellas to protect those expensive wedding outfits. Don't be afraid to ask guests to wear a pair of wellies or flat shoes; or if stilettos are a must, provide guests with heel stoppers to ensure they don't sink into the grass.

Plan for wind

It is likely that most days you will have some wind to deal with. Just make sure that any floral displays and your seating plan are well secured. Wind can be noisy so if you are having an outdoor ceremony you may want to think about using a microphone so that everyone can hear the 'I do's'.

Keeping your nan warm

For most British evenings even throughout the summer you may find a bit of a chill towards the end of the night. It is a good idea to provide a basket full of blankets.

Photo credit: Matt Brown Photography

Those pesky flies

There is nothing worse than ending up with uninvited guests at your wedding. Why not use some citronella candles or homemade wasp traps to keep them away. Consider having a net or cover for your cake or any sweet stuff. If your venue is located near a lake or water, you may want to provide mosquito repellent just in case.

TOP TIP
Don't spend time stressing about the weather, you can't control it so let it be!

Whatever happens, this is your wedding day so enjoy it. Always turn the weather into a positive, for example, why not tie ribbon to your outdoor seating or use pinwheels to provide a stunning sight when that wind does blow you could even provide bubbles instead of confetti. These types of ideas will make the day even more unique and memorable.

What You Need

* Old wax candles, or any type of safely meltable wax
* Crayons (for colouring the wax)
* Double container for melting wax (saucepan with glass measuring jug inside)
* Wicks (available at craft stores)
* Citronella oil
* Thermometer
* Old jam jars or tin cans
* Hot glue or strong tape

Citronella Candle Recipe

1. Clean out your jars and tin cans. dry completely.
2. Put your saucepan on the hob with some water and your glass measuring jug inside it.
3. Attach your wick bases to the bottom centre of your jars and tins with hot glue or tape.
4. When the water is 60°C, put your wax inside the measuring jug. stir as it starts to melt, add your crayons as well to colour.
5. When all the wax is melted to an even liquid (it will look like the consistency of olive oil), add a few drops of citronella oil and stir (about one drop for a small candle, two to three for larger ones).
6. Remove the container and pour into your jam jars, leaving about a centim of wick exposed.
7. Let it cool.

Photo credit: Chris Terry Photography

The Wedding PLANNER

7. The wedding planner

Planning a wedding can be a stressful time, let's remember you haven't done this before, so with the help of the award winning Val Mattinson from Benessamy Weddings & Events we explore the benefits of having a wedding planner to help combat the overwhelm.

Over to Val;

Why hire a planner for your wedding?

For a lot of people planning their wedding is one of the most stressful times of their life. You may not be feeling stressed yet but actually a lot of clients that I work with admit to experiencing stress unlike anything they have felt before, and that includes; changing jobs, moving house or even having children.

Sometimes it is because they have never planned anything like this before and it is something you have to do on top of your every day, so for many people, still working, still trying to run a household, trying to live a normal life and still trying to see friends and family. You are not going to cut yourself off while you plan your wedding, it's lots of juggling, lots of booking, lots of organising and it is everything on top of your day to day tasks.

So how can a wedding planner help with the stress element?

I would say from a personal point of view as a planner I like to bring calm to a client. Lots of my clients will say "actually I am fine at the moment, but I know that I will get to the point when things will unravel due to work or some major decision I've been asked to make and that I won't feel like I have got the time to do".

You may be thinking, "I got engaged, it's amazing, it's exciting but actually I've got no idea where to start".

Having a planner will help you at the beginning to make sense of it all as there are countless blogs, magazines and lots of inspiration but you might find

Photo credit: Richard Murgatroyd Photography

it just a bit daunting. Some couples do not know where to start to actually discount some of those things that everyone has suggested or venues you should visit. A planner can help give you the clarity to say 'it might not be for me'.

What are the signs to say it is possibly time to get a planner involved

Pulling hair out! Literally sitting there with your head in your hands, I have seen that. I think if you find that you have lot of things such as emails in your inbox

or post piled up that you know you need to make a decision on, if you are not replying to them then that is a sign that you perhaps need someone to help you understand what the content is all about and to help you to make that decision. It is human nature, I think a lot of people do this when dealing with tough decisions and that feeling of overwhelm is not a great one to have.

Another sign is if you're spending too much of your time planning your wedding to the detriment of everything else that's been going on in your life. This might be time to get some help or at least to find out about the help available. I can help you at the beginning of your wedding planning or if things become too much, I offer a rescue package to help you complete your plans and pull everything together. I have clients who come and say this is much more involved or this is much more complicated than I thought and I feel I am being forced to make decisions that I don't feel comfortable with. A planner can provide support and help you to make those decisions.

How can a wedding planner help you?

After giving one of my clients a long list of things to do and think about, she emailed back to say "thank you for clearing the fog" so in short I can help you to demystify everything really.

Sometimes it is that kick-starting of your plans. You may have been involved in a wedding, you may have even helped along the way if you were a bridesmaid or as a wedding guest but most of our clients have not planned a wedding before and it is that experience that will make the difference.

I am an independent wedding planner and I am here to give independent advice. I am an impartial spare pair of hands and spare pair of ears! I'm also very good at negotiation on behalf of clients so if there is something you want to find out more information about or you want to go back to a supplier and unpick some of the small print I am there to do that on your behalf.

But my friend has planned a wedding before and I think she will be fine as my wedding planner

Well what i would say to you is, whilst she has planned her wedding before or someone else's, this is YOUR wedding. As an experienced wedding planner I have skills and experience gained from planning lots of weddings. During your wedding planning I'm sure you will hear lots of advice, some will be great, some, not so great. Sometimes it is good to have someone

Photo credit: Amy Shore Photography

TOP TIP

Take the time to plan your wedding. We took 18 months to plan our perfect day, this meant some of the stress was removed, we could spread the cost and it didn't take over our lives. Don't neglect other things you have to do, its not all about the wedding!

Photo credit: Richard Murgatroyd Photography

independent and unbiased to go to and say, "I am thinking about this, what do you think?" You may have help from family and friends during your planning but sometimes you really need to have someone who is independent and who you can ask "what do you think? Do I really need to do have this or to pay for that? Is that expensive and do we need to be spending more or less on that?"

So how should you choose your planner?

Like any of the suppliers you choose to be part of your wedding day you should select a planner with great care. You should always ask them for evidence of the experience they have of planning weddings (preferably more than one at a time – It's one thing to plan your own wedding and quite another to be able to manage a number of client weddings over a sustained period of time!).

A good wedding planner should offer you a chance to meet with them before you book with them. It sounds obvious but not all planners offer this and some charge you for that meeting! I always offer an initial complimentary consultation as I think it is important for you to get to meet me, find out about the services I offer and to see if you would like to work with me. It's a great opportunity

to ask me questions and to find out about the types of weddings I have planned before, what I have got coming up and what are my ways of working such as how I keep up with current trends in the industry and what contacts I've got with suppliers and venues.

What questions should you ask your planner?

You should always understand the basis on which they work, their fee structure, what is included in the amount they quote, what is not included and what facilities they have to add things on if you need it later. I think you should always make sure that your planner has appropriate levels of insurance.

The benefit of having wedding insurance

I always advise my clients to take out wedding insurance. It can cover a range of eventualities. Think about if you had to change the date for any reason, it may be that you have already paid a deposit, you may be able to transfer this to another date, but if you have booked a supplier based on a particular date and they can't now do the new date, you might find yourself in a position where you have lost that deposit or at least part of it.

Wedding insurance is actually relatively inexpensive but it covers you for those sorts of eventualities. It can also cover you if a supplier goes out of business.

How can a planner help on the day

I never refer to it as 'on the day coordination', because even if what you are looking for is that type of support at the very end of your planning, very rarely will it just be on the day, and for me as a planner giving you the best advice for something like a tipi or marquee you need someone to help to communicate with your suppliers, in the run up to your wedding day. In the week leading up to the wedding I will be there on site to meet and liaise with suppliers and also to make sure you have a contact person that knows the set up and everything that is going on.

Photo credit: Matt Brown Photography

The best way to describe me on the day is I am your wedding day personal assistant. I am there to make sure that if you need something, you have it! Someone to handle any issues or queries that may come up. For example, if there is someone on Table 3 who wants an extra bottle of wine and the extras have already been used, I can sort this out for you because we've already had the conversation about extras, so this will let you get on and enjoy your day.

Val's final tips;

- Remember, this is YOUR wedding day. Keep that in your head throughout your wedding planning and when speaking to your venue and wedding suppliers.

- Only do what you are comfortable with and what you are happy with, keeping in mind what you definitely don't want.

- And assume any day you choose it might rain so plan for that. Then if it does you already know what you are going to do; you already have a Plan B.

LOVE IS IN THE AIR

UP, UP AND AWAY!

CAKE

83

FEEDING your Guests

8. Feeding Your Guests

When having an outdoor celebration there really are no set rules, this is the same for catering and feeding your guests.

Often couples prefer a more relaxed approach to the catering, with sharing platters served early afternoon with a bbq served in the evening. You have the freedom to do what you want to do and design the day you want to have.

Along with our friend Thomas The Caterer we explore exactly this, he is a dab hand at cooking in a field and loves an outdoor wedding, so much so he had one himself! Over to Thomas;

What's cooking in a field?

In short, whatever you want to be cooked can be done, Thomas the Caterer's whole business is built off one quote by the late great Walt Disney...

"IF YOU CAN DREAM IT, YOU CAN DO IT"

Walt Disney

How to choose a caterer?

First and foremost, you need to decide whether you want an off the shelf menu or a bespoke menu that reflects your own personalities as it is very different caterers that do this.

When considering your wedding caterer, ask yourself, 'do I like them' remembering that you will be working with them, and their team will be there with you on your special day. Once you have found a caterer that you like, other things to consider are: do they have a good reputation backed up by testimonials from other couples, do not be afraid to ask to see these.

You want your wedding caterer to listen to you and what YOU want and not force you into their own ideas. Their job is to take your ideas and inspiration and transform them into an awesome menu.

Visit your considered wedding caterer at their premises where they will be preparing your food, this will give you the opportunity to ensure that they have a clean working environment reinforced by a 5-star food hygiene rating (4 stars just won't cut it).

Scribble Space

Questions you should be asking your caterer?

Firstly, after asking yourself "Do you like them"? consider the following:

- Do they have a 5-star food hygiene rating?
- Do they have testimonials from past clients?
- Will they allow a visit to their kitchen/ preparation area?
- Have they cooked in a field before?
- Do they do tasting events and when?
- Are their menus pre written or are they bespoke?
- Do they source quality local produce?

Photo credit: Matt Brown Photography

How would you help a couple decide on their bespoke menu?

On an initial consultation, we would talk about everything from their coming together as a couple to the things that they are really well known for. We discuss the things that they love to eat and any little quirks.

For example, we once created Welsh Cheese and Leek Tart served on a replica of the Welsh Rugby pitch, things like that that make it fun and add a bit of theatre.

Photo credit: Matt Brown Photography

89

I always say to come prepared and armed with all the inspiration you have ever had, from the moment you thought about getting married, whether that be your own Pinterest board, bits ripped out of magazines even bring a recipe book if you need to, whatever the inspiration we can build it up from that.

What sort of food works well with an outdoor wedding?

Most things work really, what doesn't work well I think is a better question. Fish and shellfish as a main course I would avoid as they are generally not for everyone, even things like a beef wellington, if it is a windy day and the ovens have got vents at the back it can just blow the flame and take the heat out of the oven which is crucial to getting a delicious beef wellington. Most things can be achieved however, it is our problem to figure out how it is done right not yours, whatever you want we can figure out how to do it correctly in a field.

How does cooking in a field differ from cooking in a kitchen?

Well it is all prepped in the kitchen, so it is really just the finishing of the food and so we just bring everything we need to finish the menu and serve it like it has just left the kitchen.

LUCINDA

THANK YOU FOR SHARING OUR SPECIAL DAY

The Logistics, the where's, what's and how's

All of the food preparation is done in our kitchen at Thomas Towers, depending on what your menu is, we may require a catering tent, (which your tipi/marquee company can provide for you). We then transport your food seamlessly to your event. We do need good lighting and a minimum of 6-7 catering tables, (no chairs - there is no time to sit down!) again these can be provided by your tent company.

We do also need a fresh supply of potable water for cooking veg, cleaning hands, and washing cutlery that has been dropped! We understand that this is not always possible when cooking in a field, but we just need to know this information so that we can arrange our own if necessary.

The equipment is brought to site either on the day or the day before depending on your menu. We generally always bring a gas stove or even two for larger events, an oven and if things need frying we will bring the fryers or the BBQs.

At Thomas the Caterer we work on 1 event staff per 20 guests or 1 per 30 depending upon the menu and what service style you require. So for example if you had 100 guests we would generally have 5 front of house staff. Staffing is also influenced by the food you are having for example a sharing menu would need less than if you are having a plated a la carte style menu.

Our waiting staff are also on hand to serve your guests welcome drinks and canapés if you are having them.

We stay at the wedding until our job is done, that's generally when everything we have got is cleared away. We do try and take our equipment and rubbish on the night but this can depend, and occasionally this will be collected the following day.

TOP TIP
Confirm that your caterer and bartender will be taking and disposing of their rubbish.

TOP TIP
Confirm who is providing the knife to cut your cake. Who will then cut this up and then serve it.

TOP TIP

Check when your caterer and bar company are collecting their equipment as this will need to be cleared out of the catering tent before your tent provider arrives to dismantle.

Photo credit: Matt Brown Photography

Is your caterer providing?

- Event staff

- Crockery, cutlery

- Glassware

- Table linen

- Napkins

- Cooking equipment

- A knife to cut the cake

- Spare cutlery and crockery

Catering timeline for the day?

Initial preparations for your timeline are done when you book, finalising it all three weeks before the big day. We will sit with you and plan your timeline. This allows us to plan the structure of the day. For instance if you are getting married at 2pm and your evening guests are coming at 6pm, there is a lot to do in those 4 hours. We will plan and decide how many canapés you need, whether you want two courses, or if you prefer to have more canapés instead of a starter and then a main course. We work back to make sure it all fits in.

Your Wedding Day Catering Bible

A good caterer will produce a working document which is like the bible for the day, so even if the person that has directed your event isn't there, they have all the information in front of them that they need to know. It has everything from the event date, the couple's names, names of any key members of the party and their telephone numbers, the menu, timings down to the button (including when the guests will arrive), set up times, serving time and finishing time.

It also includes notes about special requirements, allergies or dietary requirements and whether staff meals are to be provided.

Photo credit: Chris Terry Photography

Thomas's final tips;

- Check your suppliers' contracts to see if they do or don't need a meal. People like your photographer who are there all day should and also deserve a meal!

- Spend as much as you can on your caterer, people always remember bad food at a wedding!

- For evening food, go for something that will please the masses, that is quick to serve and everyone loves. Try to make it a bit different though, a great buffet is a great buffet!

- Don't overdo it, keep it simple.

For more inspiration on wedding food ideas why not check out Thomas The Caterers book, The Definitive Guide to Wedding Food Thats Loved by Everyone.

Photo credit: Richard Murgatroyd Photography

WATERING your Guests

9. Watering your guests

There are different options for how you water your guests and doing it yourself is obviously one but this does also mean a lot of extra work and planning.

The Options

Your options for watering your guests are;

1. Employ the services of a professional bartender.
2. Run your own bar.

Employing the services of a professional bartender

These can provide for you the physical bar structure, refrigeration, your drink and trained staff together with being able to operate a cash bar service.

Consider what is important to you when you book your bartender. Is it the price of drinks? A bar company that charge less for their drinks may keep their costs down by using plastic glasses.

A bartender may be happy for you to provide all of the alcohol and just serve it for you. However this may not be the cheapest option.

Help Yourself!

Photo credit: Matt Brown Photography

Running your own bar

If you decide to run the bar yourself, source your drinks on a sale or return basis as it is very likely that you will over order. Why? Well it must be everyone's fear that they will run out of drink before the night is over!

Glassware

Glassware can be hired in at a cost. However your catering company may be able to source these for you.

When hiring in glassware make sure you confirm whether it can be returned dirty, the last thing you want to do is have to wash 300 glasses the day after your wedding.

Ikea glasses are very reasonably priced, it may work out viable to buy your glasses from there, even if it is just your wine glasses.

With a recent trend in serving drinks in jam jars, why not label a jam jar and everyone has the same glass for the day. You could serve cold beers from large ice buckets.

TOP TIP

Some supermarkets such as Sainsbury's and Waitrose provide a free glass loan service, just pay a deposit and take the glasses for up to 7 days. All you pay for are the breakages!

 Scribble Space

As easy as it all sounds you need to ask yourself the following:

- Do you need a bar structure? £cost
- Do you need glassware? £cost
- Who will serve your welcome drinks?
- Who will serve the drinks with your main meal?
- Do you need to hire in staff or will it be a free for all?
- How will the drinks stay cool? Do you need fridges or a chiller? Who will bring the ice?
- How are you getting the drinks to site and where are you storing them? Who will take the glasses back after the wedding?

TOP TIP

For us hiring a chiller was a last minute decision, as it seemed quite expensive, however it was a total lifesaver, we would have been lost without it. We did our own bar, table flowers and pudding table, the chiller allowed us to set up the days leading up to the wedding, lock everything in there and keep it all cool.

We put all of our drinks in there, as well as the flowers to keep them from wilting.

STYLING

10. Styling

The beauty of having an outdoor wedding is that it provides you with a blank canvas to style your day to reflect your own personalities.

Your options for styling are to;

- do it yourself

- dry hire from a stylist/prop hire company

- employ the services of a stylist.

Along with stylist Tara Knott from Tickety Boo Events we explore these options.

Do It Yourself

Do it yourself can be great fun and you may find talent in family and friends you never knew existed. There are some great resources out there for ideas, Pinterest obviously being one and lots of how-to videos on YouTube. My advice for this option is to be realistic with what you are capable of doing and do not underestimate the amount of work involved. If you are going to be doing this give yourself plenty of time to make things as they always take longer than you anticipate. Purchasing the materials to make items may seem like a good idea and it may feel like you are helping the budget but this can work out less cost effective than dry hiring from a stylist/prop hire company.

Dry Hire

Prop hire is a great in-between option of doing it yourself and having a stylist do it all for you. As a stylist I do offer a dry hire service, you are welcome to visit the studio to see items that are available to hire and I can make recommendations to you of items that will work together and enhance the look you are going for.

These can be collected a few days before your big day or delivered subject to the distance you are getting married.

TOP TIP
Allocate a budget for styling even if you intend to do it all yourself!

Photo credit: Richard Murgatroyd Photography

Using a Stylist

My favorite option is working with you to style your event space.

This provides me with an opportunity to find out more about you as a couple, how you met, what your interests are, what your tastes are and what kind of décor you like. By working together I can ensure that your own personalities are brought to life in the styling.

The next step is to build upon this, I would always recommend starting with a colour scheme that you want for your wedding which really is a personal choice, this could be influenced by the time of year for example

Photo credit: Richard Murgatroyd Photography

you may have a particular flower in mind to use or even certain fabrics. My advice with your colour scheme is to consider your event space too for example golds would look great in a marquee against the white, but against the canvas of a tipi it can become lost.

As a couple you need to incorporate your personality into the styling as this is what makes it unique. We would start this off by drawing up a list of what you like and what you really do not like. I am styling a wedding this year where the couple are really into their music and so we are incorporating this into the centre pieces and table plan.

My next job as a stylist is to help by bringing all of the ideas together. Armed with details of your own personal touches, colour pallet and a particular theme, (for example a rustic look or a contemporary feel) I would then create an inspiration board as an initial start to work from, via a secret Pinterest board.

Whichever option you decide works for you regarding styling one tip I have for you is to have a cut off time for ideas. Pinterest, Instagram and magazines are great for inspiration but you also need to reach a point where you stop looking and are happy with the choices you have made, otherwise you can keep going and going with ideas and this can become overwhelming.

 Scribble Space

The benefit of having a stylist, in addition to having an expert on hand, is that it saves you work. It is my job to bring all of the styling items to site and set them up, giving you the time to get ready for your big day, plus I will also take it all down the day after. The last thing you want to do the day after getting married is get up and start having to take candles and décor down.

TOP TIP

Where you can, make things yourself. Small personal details make for a more memorable wedding. If you are making elements of your wedding don't leave it too late. We made lots over the winter months to get ahead of the game.

How should you choose your stylist

Obviously you have got to like the work that they do and you can get an insight for this on their website, Instagram and Pinterest. Also I think you have to be able to work together, choosing someone that listens to you and isn't just pushing their own ideas. The end result has to be what you the couple want.

When should you get a stylist onboard?

The earlier you get a stylist onboard, the better. This gives time for us to work together building on your ideas, especially if you have a bigger event space when more time is appreciated. The reality is I have prepared and styled weddings with as little as seven weeks lead time and others over a year.

"If you're doing your own flowers visit a wholesale market. Flowers are not cheap but we knew we would get more flowers for our money by doing the table and venue decorations ourselves. We had a proper practice a couple of weeks before the wedding so we could see how they would work and to see how many days each type of flower took to open up".

Photo credit: Yvonne Lishman Photography

111

How do you spot trends

I actually look at a lot of house interior magazines and blogs, or online like Pinterest and Instagram. Depending on what I am looking for I just start by searching key words **#centrepieces #vintagewedding #coppercandles** and that will pull up lots of things, and there are also certain Instagram accounts I would follow. Green Wedding Shoes is one of my favourites as they have so many ideas and then there are lots of house interior accounts that I follow – it is really interesting to see how fashion, interiors and textiles all flow through to weddings and the impact it has on the style.

I always set up a Pinterest board with couples so we can both pin to it, but I do use Instagram a lot for inspiration.

DIY styling on site check list;

(Great for hanging things)
* String/Floristry Twine
* Fishing line
* Cable ties

(Other useful tools)
* Scissors
* Drawing pins

- Glue gun
- Safety pins
- Needle and cotton
- Ladders
- Cutting Pliers
- Safety matches (for candles)

Cable ties and fishing wire will become your best friend when styling your space. Both are perfect for securing items such as bunting, lanterns and pom poms and even to secure your seating plan to your easel. They are also easily cut after the day for a quick clear up operation.

Photo credit: Yvonne Lishman Photography

Ceremony
OPTIONS

11. Ceremony Options

There really is nothing more beautiful than an outdoor wedding ceremony, but unfortunately there are a few legal limitations to this (in England and Wales). Hopefully these will change in years to come but at the moment the Marriage and Civil Partnerships Regulations state that marriages can only take place within a permanently immovable structure comprising at least a room or any boat or other vessel which is permanently moored. Any premises outside this definition, such as the open air, a tent, marquee or any other temporary structure and most forms of transport are not permitted.

In short, this means a no to getting married in a tipi or marquee in England and Wales (the rules are different in Scotland)

However, all is not lost, you could still have your perfect outdoor wedding by having a blessing or humanist ceremony, giving you the freedom to have your wedding where you want. This means the location can be in the field you always walk the dog in, or the tipis you have fallen in love with. Unfortunately, though these are not technically legal, so it does require you to do what we like to call 'the paperwork'. Many couples attend the registry office a few days before their wedding day to complete 'the paperwork'. The outdoor blessing on your wedding day is then considered to be the actual

Photo credit: Yvonne Lishman Photography

wedding ceremony and most guests will never even know the difference. By doing this, it allows you to hold the outdoor ceremony the way that you choose to, reflecting your own beliefs and style.

With the great British weather it is always advisable to have a contingency plan. If it is a rainy day, this is unlikely to last the whole day and so you may be able to hang on a short time to wait for the storm to pass, but failing this you could relocate your guests into your tipi/marquee.

Having your ceremony conducted by a Celebrant means that you have the freedom to express your vows to each other in your own words, and choose readings and music which mean something to you as a couple.

If you have decided on an outdoor ceremony this will need to be set up on the morning. Consider who will be doing this:

- Land owner/venue
- Groom/groomsmen
- Family & friends
- Stylist

Realistically you do not need anything to make your outdoor ceremony work, but of course you are going to want to make the area look pretty and look like it is set for the purpose of holding a ceremony.

Consider where you will host the ceremony, this may be obvious but if not look for an imposing tree, a quirky wall or something that provides a stunning backdrop. Next think about how you will approach the ceremony area and can you clearly identify your aisle.

Set out the seating for your guests, what are they going to sit on?

Straw bales are a perfect base for your seating however they can be prickly or irritate some people. You can hire or make covers for them or even use blankets. Remember guests may be wearing delicate fabrics and do not want to be snagging their new dresses on the straw.

You may consider that not all guests want to sit on straw bales so you may have some chairs or benches just in

Photo credit: Camera Hannah Photography

case. You could use these from your tipi/marquee, confirm this is ok with your furniture supplier

Think about where you will stand. Will you be standing for the whole ceremony? It may last for around 20 minutes so standing shouldn't be too difficult. Some Celebrants still have a register for you to sign so a small table and a couple of chairs works well. If there is no natural backdrop you can create your own very simply. This could be a job for your stylist or time for you to get creative. A search for 'outdoor ceremony' on Pinterest will give you plenty of ideas!

Finally, dont forget your plan B. In case of bad weather have an alternative area undercover that you can move to if required. This may be inside the tipis or marquee.

Confetti

Most guests forget to bring confetti so why not create a confetti bar or a basket of confetti cones? Remember you are in the natural environment so be considerate to the style of confetti you use.

Photo credit: Yvonne Lishman Photography

The FINAL Countdown

12. The Final Countdown

Whoop, here it is your final few days before you tie the knot. It's time for all of your planning and ideas to finally come together and share your day with family and friends.

This is going to be a busy few days and there is one key word to help you, DELEGATION.

Timeline for the day

THURSDAY

Structure Set up

Generator arrives

Event planner on site

Handover (begin to bring things to site)

FRIDAY

Toilets arrive

Caterers set up

Bar company set up

Styling

Camping tents erected

SATURDAY

Wedding Day

SUNDAY

Breakfast & BBQ

Tidy up day

Structure dismantled

The above timeline gives you an idea of what will be happening in these last few days.

Wednesday/Thursday. Your structure arrives. Although you will have already agreed with your structure company where your tipi/marquee will be going it is always nice to be around when they first set up. You will be able to confirm 100% that you are happy where it is located. If you have a wedding planner as part of their service they should also be on site to welcome your suppliers and ensure that everything is being set up and positioned where agreed.

The set up should take between 1-2 days and will be handed over to you by the Thursday evening. On the handover have a couple of key people with you to be your eyes and ears so they can also take on board the information you are provided, but remember ultimately this is your responsibility. At handover also ensure you understand how the generator works, how to monitor the fuel level and top it up with diesel if required.

Thursday may also be the day that you actually get married if you are having an outdoor ceremony (England and Wales only) or having your rehearsal at the church.

Use the Thursday to do the running around, collecting glassware, printing off your final seating plan, remember to print a copy for your caterers too. Print off your supplier list and key wedding party members' contact details and distribute these.

Friday. This is your day to bring all your creative ideas together and finally see your Pinterest board come to life. If you have a stylist doing this for you, run through with them one last time where things will be going and you can now take the time to go and get pampered. If however you have opted for a more DIY approach, now is the time to rope in the help of family and friends.

Delegation

Make sure you have list of what needs completing. Pass this responsibility to family and friends, as they will all want to be part of your day and have no doubt been asking how they can be involved. Today is the day to let them. Ideally start with hanging decorations as this can involve moving furniture around so it is always best done before the tables are set.

TOP TIP

Jobs you could delegate include:
- Hanging items
- Collecting table linen or glassware
- Setting up displays
- Preparing the guest book
- Creating the photo booth
- Setting out external seating areas
- Hanging ribbon and lights in trees
- Putting out solar lights for walkways

TOP TIP

Outdoor games are a great way to get your guests interacting and gives you time out for photos together.

Outdoor games

Having outdoor games at your wedding is a great way to have fun and pull all of your guests together. There are so many great ideas for outdoor wedding games.

- Tin can alley – Empty bean tins covered in washi tape looks really effective.
- Tic Tac Toe – Pebbles painted with a board marked out with tape or paint.
- Wellie wanging – use flags as markers
- Cricket
- Limbo
- Hoopla – Washed out beer bottles and tapestry hoops
- Frisby
- Dominoes
- Giant Ker Plunk
- Giant Jenga
- Connect 4
- Coconut shy
- Skittles
- Space hoppers
- Sack race
- Apple bobbing

> **TOP TIP**
> Straw bales are a good addition to your games area and can be used to create the skittles alley for example.

Some games can be hired but for very little outlay and a lot of fun you can make some of them yourself. Try looking on Pinterest for more inspiration.

Wedding Day

Most of all, what you need to remember about today is that it is all about the two of you, celebrating in an awesome way with your nearest and dearest.

To ensure that this day kicks off in the right way there will no doubt be a few last minute jobs, that couldn't have been done until this point.

These final jobs will include putting out road signs to help guests get to site, setting up your ceremony area and table settings. For table settings, create a mock up before the day and photograph this. Show who will be laying these exactly how you want it to look. If you are having lots of candles on the day, think about who will light them. If you have used the generator before the big day, check the generator fuel level.

Wedding day management

If you have a wedding planner providing wedding day management, as part of their role they will be on site in the morning to receive your suppliers. If, however you have chosen not to use a wedding planner and your venue does not offer any kind of assistance with on-the-day management then you will need to consider who will be receiving your suppliers such as your florist, caterers, bartenders, stylist and cake supplier plus who will complete your final tasks.

TOP TIP
Don't forget to
cut the cake!

Photo credit: Yvonne Lishman Photography

TOP TIP

Enjoy every minute as it goes really fast. Take time out with your bride/groom every hour to remember what you are celebrating.

Photo credit: Shoot It Momma Photography

Timeline for the day

Having an outdoor tipi/marquee wedding lends itself to being more relaxed than a conventional wedding. The timescales for the day should be no different, however there are elements that will need to be considered.

What time are you getting married? This can then influence how many times you have to feed your guests. For a later wedding at around 4pm, you would only need to feed your guests once, for an earlier 1pm ceremony, you will need to provide a meal for your day guests and then food for your evening guests.

A typical timeline would be:

> **1pm ceremony**
> **3pm Speeches and food**
> **7pm Evening guests arrive**
> **8:30-9pm Evening food**

There is plenty of time in between for photos, games and catching up with guests.

These timings will be crucial to your caterer in order to feed your guests at the right time. This will be discussed in your catering meeting and can also be used to share with your other suppliers. i.e. band, magician etc.

TOP TIP

Relax, it will be the best day of your life. Make sure you dance, savour the food and enjoy all of the memories you are making and all of the hard work you have put in.

"On the day we had a wedding planner. I met up with her once a month before the wedding and the day before. She was great for pulling things together at the last minute. She kept the running of the day to time and coordinated all of the suppliers. She was our go to lady if any of us had a problem, e.g. we did all of the table wines ourselves, but as the food was coming out we forgot we'd left it in the chiller, as it was a warm day. She quickly sorted these little glitches out for us".

TOP TIP

Having a BBQ the day after allowed us to see all of our guests who stayed nearby overnight. We took everything we needed before the wedding, so it was just a case of turning up the day after the wedding and welcoming everyone. The only thing is the charm certainly wasn't the same the morning after the night before, but it didn't take long for a few of us to tidy up.

Photo credit: Matt Brown Photography

The following day

If you and your guests have camped over or stayed close by, make arrangements to get together the following morning for brunch or maybe even a fun game of rounders! This is a great way to see your guests once more before they travel home and extends your wedding celebrations. Whilst your friends and family are with you they could help with any of the tidying away that may be needed before you hand the tipi/marquee back.

Help could include:

• Removal of personal belongings

• Removal of presents/gifts

• Removal of styling items

• Removal of rubbish

This does need some thought and planning too. It might be that you arrange for the local breakfast van to deliver breakfast rolls for everyone to make things easier.

Last Word

You chose to have this style wedding as you wanted something more relaxed and in keeping with your own style. Whatever happens embrace every moment and enjoy it, it will be your perfect day.

Start your Wedding Planning Here

12 - 18 months

- Choose Your wedding Date ☐
- Write your guest list ☐
- Create a budget ☐
- Decide on must haves and would likes ☐
- Have the money chat with family ☐
- Purchase wedding insurance ☐
- Book venue/site ☐
- Book tipi/marquee company ☐
- Secure church/ceremony ☐
- Diarise wedding open days ☐
- Send out Save the dates ☐

10 months

- Hire wedding planner ☐
- Book caterer ☐
- Chose bridal party ☐
- Consider accommodation ☐
- Book band/music ☐
- Book photographer (have engagement shoot) ☐
- Book videographer ☐

1 month

- Purchase drinks (if you are doing your own bar) ☐
- Purchase wedding favours ☐
- Collect Dress ☐

Save the date

2 weeks

- Make timescales for day before ☐
- Agree who is returning hire items ☐
- Delegate tasks ☐
- Collect wedding rings ☐

1 week

- Pack everything you are taking to site including tool kit and decoration items ☐
- Make sure groomsmen have important numbers ☐
- Collect suits ☐

8 months

- Book stylist ☐
- Book florist ☐
- Choose your wedding cake ☐
- Begin honeymoon planning ☐

6 months

- Book additional food suppliers (ice cream van/pizza van/crepe van) ☐
- Book your wedding night accommodation ☐
- Begin DIY making ☐
- Book any additional entertainment (magician etc) ☐
- Book bartenders ☐
- Book transportation ☐
- Meet with tipi/marquee company to discuss layouts ☐
- Finalise wedding suits/dress/designer wellies! ☐
- Book your utilities (toilets/generator) ☐

2 months

- Final planning meeting with tipi/marquee company ☐

4 months

- Ring shopping ☐
- Send invitations ☐
- Hair and makeup trial ☐

48 hours

- Pick up glassware ☐

The Big Day

Budget Planner

Budget Item	Budgeted Amount	Actual Cost	Deposit Paid	Outstanding Balance	Due Date
The Big Ones					
Land Hire					
Tipi/Marquee					
Catering					
Honeymoon					
Ceremony/Church					
Utilities					
Generator					
Toilets					
Heater					
Suppliers					
Wedding Planner					
Flowers					
Styling					
Photographer					
Videographer					
Apparel					
Wedding Dress					
Suits					
Rings					

Budget Item	Budgeted Amount	Actual Cost	Deposit Paid	Outstanding Balance	Due Date
Pretty Bits					
Flowers					
Styling					
Cake					
Favours					
Hair/Makeup					
Special Touches					
Stationery					
On the Day					
Transportation					
Accommodation					
Bar/Drinks					
Gifts					
Band					
Disco/DJ					
Other Entertainment					
Other Items					
Hen Do					
Stag Do					
Insurance					

Supplier	Contact Name	Telephone	Email
SamiTipi	Jodie	01332 806040	events@samitipi.co.uk

Supplier	Contact Name	Telephone	Email

Scribble Space

ACKNOWLEDGMENTS

Wedding Suppliers
Industry expertise and knowledge provided by:
Sami Tipi – samitipi.co.uk
Thomas the Caterer - thomasthecaterer.co.uk
Val Mattinson – Benessamy Weddings & Events benessamy.co.uk
Tara Knott – Tickety Boo Events ticketybooevents.co.uk

Wedding Suppliers
Featured in the photos and part of our journey:
Lynne & Richard Bailey - Bawdon Lodge Farm bawdonlodgefarm.co.uk
Jo Clarke – My Perfect Ceremony myperfectceremony.co.uk
Clare McCabe – Purple Star Design purplestardesign.co.uk
Mainline Plant Hire - mainline-hire.co.uk
Mambo Mobile Bars - mambomobilebars.co.uk
Darby and Joan - darbyandjoanvintage.co.uk
Tineke Floral Designs - tinekefloraldesigns.co.uk
Doris Loves - dorisloves.co.uk
Honey Bees Vintage Teas - honeybeesvintageteas.co.uk
Bell Bliss – bellbliss.co.uk
Kniftons - kniftonsmobiletoilets.co.uk
Cars of Derby - weddingcarsofderby.co.uk
Best Day Ever - bestdayeveruk.com
Yummy Little Cakes - yummylittlecakes.co.uk
Jo Beth Floral Design - jo-bethfloral.co.uk
Polly and Me - pollyandme.bigcartel.com
Natural Favours - naturalfavours.com
Vintage Caravan Booth - vintage-booth.co.uk
The White Bulb Company - thewhitebulb.com

Bennaberry Products - benaberry.weebly.com
The Little Camion Creperie - tlccreperie.com
Stuart Carter - stuartcarter.co.uk
Button of Love
Hayley Angell and Lisa Harris
Amy & Matt Baxter
Mark Skorupa and Chris Sutton

Photographers
Stunning photographs were taken by the talented:
Chris Terry - christopherterryweddings.co.uk
Matt Brown - mattbrownphotography.co.uk
Yvonne Lishman - yvonnelishmanphotography.co.uk
Alexandra Jane - alexandrajane.co.uk
Richard Murgatroyd - richardmurgatroyd.com
Camera Hannah – camerahannah.co.uk
Shoot it Momma - shootitmomma.co.uk
Amy Shore - amyshorephotography.com

The ones who have
Real experience tips were provided by:
Annabel & Chris Parkinson-Lee
Siobhan & Mike Ludlow
Lisa & Mark Matthews
Samantha & Tom Sullivan
Kayleigh & Dan Packwood
Dani & Jords Brown